You Are My Miracle

MARYANN CUSIMANO LOVE

illustrated by SATOMI ICHIKAWA

SCHOLASTIC INC.

New York Toronto London Auckland Sydney
Mexico City New Delhi Hong Kong Buenos Aires

ISBN-13: 978-0-439-93324-7
ISBN-10: 0-439-93324-2

12 11 10 9 10 11/0

Printed in the U.S.A. 40

First Scholastic printing, December 2006

Design by Gunta Alexander

Text set in Post Mediaeval

The art was painted in watercolor on Fabriano paper.

To Maria and Rich, my miracles—M.C.L.

To Stella—S.I.

I am your parent;
you are my child.
I am your quiet place;
you are my wild.

MERRY
Welcome!

I am your hot cocoa;
you are my marshmallow.
I am your nutcracker;
you are my cookie dough.

I am your gingerbread;
you are my frosting goo.
I am your paper;
you are my glitter and glue.

I am your wrapping;
you are my surprise.

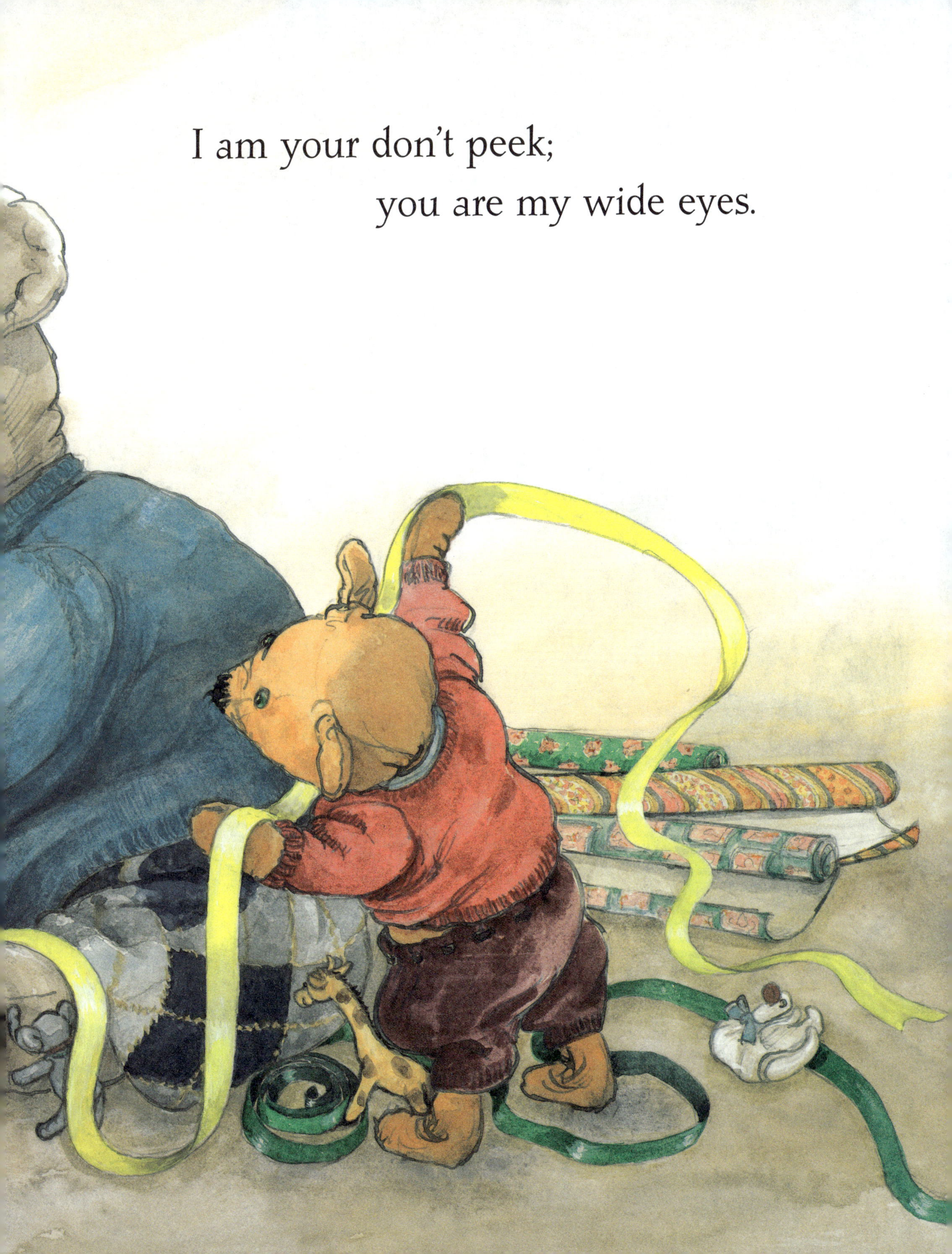

I am your don't peek;

you are my wide eyes.

I am your bundle up;
you are my dash outside.
I am your uphill pull;
you are my fast sleigh ride.

I am your fortress;

you are my snowball fight.

I am your decorate;

you are my tangled lights.

I am your helper;
you are my do-it-myself.
I am your Santa Claus;
you are my Christmas elf.

I am your glass ball;
you are my popcorn strings.
I am your pageant;
you are my angel's wings.

I am your steady hands;
you are my rising star.

I am your stocking;

you are my chocolate bar.

I am your caroling;
you are my jingle bell.
I am your favorite song;
you are my first noel.

I am your old stories;
you are my make-believe.
I am your go to sleep;
you are my Christmas Eve.

I am your hush now;
you are my lyrical.

I am your peace on Earth;
you are
my miracle.